The Practical Massage Therapist:

A Thoughtful Approach for the Solo Practitioner

Book One:

How Much Can I Earn as a Massage Therapist?

Rhonda Henry, LMP
practicalmt@yahoo.com

Table of Contents

Preface

My name is Rhonda Henry, and I've been doing massage for a living as a solo practitioner in a small community in Washington state since early 1998.

When I decided to go to massage school in 1997, it felt like a calling I had to answer and how much money I was going to make didn't really enter into the equation. I was newly divorced, cleaning houses for a living, and when it came to the money part, I thought that the idea of doing a few massages a day for $50 each sounded a lot better than cleaning houses for half of that – in other words, that I could perhaps make a bit more money for a bit less effort and enjoy it more besides.

It didn't take too long for me to figure out that the business part of massage was a good bit more complicated than that, and many years later, I find that there's still a lot of confusion and misinformation about the simple question of how much money you can expect to earn working for yourself as a private practice massage therapist.

I decided to begin the "Practical Massage Therapist" series with this booklet because it's become painfully clear to me that I'm not the only person who started out with no realistic idea of how much money a massage therapist can expect to earn for his or her efforts, what it actually takes to earn that money, or how much is left in your pocket for rent and food after taking care of even the most basic business expenses and taxes.

If I had a dollar for every person who told me they thought massage therapists were "raking it in", well....I wouldn't have to do massage anymore!

Questions or comments? Email: practicalmt@yahoo.com

Introduction

The earnings figures commonly available for massage therapists are don't usually include enough real world detail to provide an accurate picture of the true earning potential for a massage therapist working on his or her own in a one-person private practice.

It's all too easy to see the high hourly rates charged for massage and decide that being a massage therapist will be a great way to make $80,000 or more a year, but the truth is that most massage therapists don't get to take home anywhere near that much money.

Many massage therapists are self-employed as solo practitioners, while others work as independent contractors (or much less frequently, as actual full or part-time salaried employees) for spas, chiropractors or other businesses who hire massage therapists. Some are able to work more hours in a given period of time, others less; some live in an area where they can charge a lot per hour for their work while others can charge relatively little. Some have very high expenses associated with their work; others spend relatively little in the way of business expenses.

Even so, there are still some basic "earning principles" that are common to all massage therapists regardless of experience level or work setting. We will explore those principles one by one, then use them together in a simple worksheet format, with examples drawn from real life so that you can more easily figure out the type of earning potential that most closely matches your particular life/work circumstances.

Earning Principle #1

Earning Principle #1: There is a limit to the total number of hours it is possible for a given massage therapist to spend on both the paid and the non-paid but equally essential "administrative hours" that are part of the business of running a private massage practice.

Massage therapy is physically and at times emotionally demanding work, and it is the unusual massage therapist who is able to do much more than 20 to 25 hours per week of hands-on massage work on a regular basis without excessive fatigue or a potentially career-ending repetitive stress injury. Most professional massage organizations define full time employment for massage therapists as 15-20 hours per week of actual hands-on massage work.

When thinking about how many hours per week of massage **you** might be able to do on a regular basis, there are two major factors to consider:

1) Your overall level of health, especially how well your body adapts to physical exercise, along with any injuries or chronic conditions you might have that could affect your ability to do massage.

2) How much **total** time you can commit to your practice of massage. For every paid hour with a client, count on spending roughly another hour or so of unpaid time in non-paid administrative tasks (see Appendix A for a sample list of these activities).

As an example, someone who is just getting used to doing massage, or has only 20 hours per week total to devote to their practice might plan on a maximum of roughly 10 paid hands-on hours per week of massage and another 10 hours or so of administrative tasks.

In contrast, someone who is in very good physical condition and has a minimum of 40 hours per week total to commit to a full time practice might reasonably expect to target 20 to 25 paid client hours per week as an achievable goal once his or her practice has matured and stabilized.

Earning principle #2

Earning principle #2: Many (if not most) massage therapists will not work 52 or even 50 full weeks a year doing massage for any number of different reasons.

Not only is it physically difficult for massage therapists to work many hours for many weeks in a row without excess fatigue or increased chance of injury, there are other circumstances that can affect how many work weeks are truly available to count towards your earning potential.

Sometimes time away from paid work is planned; we may choose to take that time for ourselves, our families, our faith community or for charitable work. We may be also be required by law to take time away from work in order to accomplish hours of continuing education required to maintain our massage license and the right to practice legally.

When unpaid time is unplanned, we may miss paid work due to our own illness or that of family members, injuries that may or may not be related to doing massage, and/or various emergencies (problems with cars, homes, etc.) and/or " acts of God" (extreme weather events or other serious emergencies).

Therefore, when thinking about an accurate estimate of what kind of earnings to expect as a massage therapist, we not only need to take into account how much massage we can physically accomplish in a given week, but, how many weeks a year we are actually available to carry out those hours of paid massage.

Personal needs and circumstances can and do vary quite widely, so, as a starting point, I suggest that five weeks be subtracted from the 52 weeks available to work , i.e., two weeks for vacation time and/or general family needs, another week for significant holidays where you and/or your clients may be out of town and/or too busy with other activities to schedule or receive massage (Christmas, Easter, July 4th, Thanksgiving, etc), a week for planned time away from the office (continuing education, professional or community meetings, etc), and, another week for unplanned time (illnesses, family emergencies, etc.) for a total of about five weeks away from paid work, or, a potential maximum of 47 paid weeks of massage availability per year.

Earning Principle #3

Earning principle #3: Maximum potential annual earning hours can be calculated by multiplying estimated paid hours worked per week times estimated number of work weeks available per year.

If you've followed along this far, good! We now have a good idea of how many hours a week it's generally possible to do the paid work of massage as well as how many weeks a year we are truly available to work, and as a result of those two things, we're closer to to being able to estimate a realistic annual maximum earning potential for a hypothetical massage therapist.

As an example, then, if we were to assume that a hypothetical massage therapist is physically able to work an average of 20 hours per week, and, we further assume that he or she is available to work about 47 weeks per year as described above, that provides a potential maximum of about 940 paid hours of massage work per year (20 x 47 = 940).

In theory, all we need to do now is choose an appropriate hourly rate for massage therapy, multiply that hourly rate by those 940 hours, and, we'll have a number that reflects the potential maximum annual amount a massage therapist can earn, prior to subtracting business expenses and any required local, state and federal taxes.

But, there's one more factor to consider, i.e., about how many of those available 940 hours we can actually expect to fill with paying clients day after day, week after week, and month after month; while it would be wonderful to fill every single one of those hours with paying clients, the truth is that it's not always as easy to do as we might like.

Even with a dedicated, consistent and effective marketing effort, great massage skills and equally great followup and customer service skills, the truth is that sometimes massage appointments just plain go unfilled; that's part of the risk we take on when we take on the challenge of the business of massage therapy – so, on to Earning Principle #4!

Earning Principle #4

Earning Principle #4: How much you can earn is directly related to how full you can keep the hours you are actually available to do massage.

That may seem pretty simple, but, remember: for most people in most situations, massage therapy is a completely voluntary, completely out of pocket expense, not an obligation like food or rent or dental bills or car repairs. Sometimes clients just decide to spend their money on other things besides massage – and when they choose to do so, it's no reflection on you on on the value of your work.

Massage clients also want to take vacations, they too have suddenly sick children or get sick themselves, they have all sorts of unplanned expenses just like you do, they get laid off from jobs, get divorced or decide to move away, and they don't usually let you know all of this far enough in advance for you to find enough replacement clients in time to keep the same amount of money coming in.

Because of all that, your appointment book can suddenly become partially to even fully empty through no fault of your own, cutting into your earning potential when you least need, expect, or want that to happen.

Since it's difficult enough to plan for the unknown in your own life, let alone in all of your client's lives, the best we can do to account for this type of risk is to try and "guesstimate" just how fully booked we can keep the hours we do have available in a given work year.

My own "guesstimate" is to plan for a work year that is about 80% full; that includes allowing for about 10% of those 940 hours for massage appointments that never fill in the first place (i.e., 94 hours), and, another 10% for appointments that are lost and unable to be filled especially when very regular clients are suddenly ill, need to leave town for family reasons, move away for a new job or go on extended vacations (another 94 hours, for a total of 188 hours).

That means that our "true" number of estimated paid hours available for a year for that hypothetical massage therapist would be roughly 80% of 940 hours, or, about 752 hours (940 hours minus 20%, or 188 hours).

We've managed to figure out a realistic number of hours that most massage therapists can work in an average week, and, more importantly, how many hours that massage therapist is likely to actually do paid work in the course of the average work year.

Now, we're almost ready to calculate gross income – which is what you earn for doing massage prior to subtracting the business related expenses incurred in generating those earnings, and, prior to subtracting any taxes you may owe on those earnings at the state, local and/or federal level.

At this point, estimating gross income should be pretty simple – just multiply the number of hours we've figured out we can actually get paid for doing massage by an appropriate hourly rate, and, voila! That's roughly how much you can expect to earn (again, prior to business expenses and taxes) in the average year of a reasonably mature massage practice (meaning that you may or may not do that well in the first year or two of a private practice).

But first, we need to talk about Earning Principle #5.....

Earning Principle #5

Earning Principle #5: There is no one particular or guaranteed hourly rate charged for massage therapy. The hourly rates charged for massage can vary widely according to local economic conditions and the experience level of the massage therapist, as well as the specific type of setting in which massage takes place.

For example, a very upscale solo practice, run by an experienced practitioner in a spa-type environment in a wealthy area may charge $150 or more for an hour of massage, while a private practitioner working in a small office on his or her own might charge as little as $25 per hour or as much as $100 or more depending on his or her location and level of experience.

Practitioners working in smaller, less wealthy communities would probably charge less for their work, while those practitioners working in urban areas with larger populations and higher levels of disposable income would be more likely to charge a higher hourly rate for massage (generally with correspondingly high expenses).

When determining an appropriate hourly rate for massage in your area, do some research and see what other practitioners are charging for comparable levels of training and experience. When you're just starting out, it's wise to charge less rather than more, both to reflect your experience level, and, to be able to give your self regular raises as your confidence, skill level and client base increases over time.

It's important to keep in mind that this average hourly rate wouldn't necessarily include any special offers or discounts, nor would it include any tips that might be received. In other words, the actual hourly rate you receive might be higher or lower depending on whether or not discounts and tips are included in that hourly figure.

Earning Principle #6

Earning Principle #6: Potential gross earnings (how much you can hope to earn, prior to subtracting business expenses and local, state and federal taxes) can be calculated by multiplying the estimated number of paid hours worked, times the usual amount charged per hour.

One commonly quoted average figure is $60 charged per hour of therapeutic massage, with no particular location, business type or experience/skill level specified; if we use that figure, we can then calculate the maximum potential earnings for our hypothetical massage therapist in solo practice to be about $45,120 in gross earnings (those 752 hours from Earnings Principle #4, multiplied by $60 for each one of those hours).

That's a pretty good annual wage, at least by some reckonings; however, before we know how much of that qualifies as "take home pay", we need to figure out some approximation of business expenses and taxes and subtract that from our gross earnings.

On to Earning Principle #7......!

Earning Principle #7

Earning Principle #7: Gross earnings is just part of the earnings picture. You still need to subtract business expenses and taxes before figuring out your take-home pay for doing massage.

With a figure of $45,120 of maximum potential gross earnings for our hypothetical massage therapist working 752 paid hours per year at $60 per hour, we need to address a few more items to understand what any gross income figure represents in terms of actual money that can be spent on groceries, rent, bills and savings for the future.

Individual situations vary widely regarding business expenses and taxes, so it's not possible to know exactly how much of that $45,120 our hypothetical massage therapist actually gets to keep without knowing more about his or her total business, financial and tax situation (which includes other family members who may be contributing taxable income to the household and thus affecting the overall tax picture, especially regarding federal taxes).

Lists of typical expenses and possible taxes for massage therapists are listed at the end of this e-booklet in Appendix B and C, but, for general purposes, we can use some rough guesses to subtract those items and calculate approximate take home pay for our hypothetical massage therapist.

A good general rule of thumb is to allow between one-third and one-half of gross income for expenses (office rent, utilities, advertising, insurance, general office expense like sheets, oils, lotions, etc.) and taxes (local, state and federal taxes, including federal self-employment tax at 15% of gross income after those expenses).

That means that our hypothetical massage therapist can expect to take home somewhere between $22,560 (1/2 of $45,120) and $30,800 (2/3 of $45,120) or so for the sum total his or her efforts, both in terms of the money paid for doing massage and the non-paid hours needed to sustain the practice as a whole.

Putting it all together

Now that we've gone over the basic earnings principles, it's time to put them together using the earnings worksheet for the case studies that follow.

I've supplied a blank version of the worksheet at the end of this booklet. Feel free to make as many copies as you need to explore as many different ways of working that interest you.

You can use that worksheet to figure out your own earning potential, but first, we'll use that worksheet along with some real life examples to get a better picture of what a massage therapist can really earn for his or her heartfelt efforts.

Note that there are many ways to do the work of massage therapy, and the sample case studies that follow are just a few examples gleaned from the experiences of therapists I've met and/or read about.

If there is a particular way of working that appeals to you above and beyond a simple one-person private practice (for example, a mobile massage practice, working as an independent contractor for a spa, gym, or chiropractor, or as part of a clinic with multiple practitioners, etc.), I would encourage you to talk to others who are doing this type of massage work, and interview them to get the information you need to fill out one or more versions of the earnings worksheet and decide if that particular path makes sense for you or not.

On to the case studies.....!

Case Study #1

In our first case study, we'll take a look at Robert, a nurse, massage therapist and father of two middle school age children, is married to an accountant and does massage from a small home office with a private entrance and it's own restroom nearby.

Robert is able to see clients for about two hours two evenings a week and is sometimes available on Saturday to see clients for up to four hours, averaging about five available client hours per week which he currently keeps about 60% full. He spends another four to six hours scheduling, documenting and promoting his small practice, mostly by visiting local fairs and markets with his massage chair along with donations to charitable functions in his community.

Robert's entire family takes a three week vacation every year and short local ski trips in the winter. Sometimes his wife is away on business and Robert is not able to see clients at all because of his temporarily increased family responsibilities; so, after a bit of head scratching to accommodate all that uncertainty, Robert figures that he is available to see clients about 44 weeks a year, assuming he stays healthy, which he usually does.

Robert has only been practicing massage for a little over a year. He lives in a small, semi-rural community that is fairly close to a larger urban area and currently charges $40 for an hour of massage which he plans to increase a little at a time as his experience and client base grows.

His business expenses are quite low for now, and include an appropriate amount for a home office deduction and proportionate use of utilities as determined with the help of the family tax adviser. He has vehicle expenses related to promoting his practice, along with insurance, massage supplies and laundry expenses. He does little or no advertising, and for the moment, has no website advertising his practice. He expects his expenses to rise as he finds more time to increase his skills with continuing education and further promote his business.

Earnings Worksheet – Case Study #1

A) Total hours available per work week: <u>10</u>

B) Estimated administrative hours:
     approximately ½ of total hours (A):   <u>5</u>

C) Massage hours available per work week:
     Total hours (A) minus admin hours (B):   <u>5</u>

D) Work weeks available per year:
     52 weeks minus vacation, sick time,
     holidays, family time, etc.   <u>44</u>

E) Total potential massage hours per year:
     Massage hours per week (C)
     multiplied by weeks available (D):   <u>220</u>

F) Estimated percent of appointments filled: <u>60</u> % x .01 = <u>.60</u>

G) Adjusted massage hours per year:
     Total potential massage hours (E)
     multiplied by (F)   <u>132</u>

H) Estimated hourly rate for massage: <u>$40</u>

I) Estimated Gross earnings:
     Adjusted massage hours (G) multiplied by
     Estimated hourly rate (H):   <u>$5280.00</u>

J) Estimated Expenses and Taxes:
     Allow for one-third to one-half of
     gross earnings for expenses and taxes: <u>$5280/3</u> = $1760

K) Estimated Net Earnings after taxes/expenses:
     Subtract Estimated Expenses/Taxes (J)
     from Estimated Gross Earnings (I):   <u>$5280 - $1760 = $3520.00</u>

Case Study #2

Our second case study is Laura, a mother of two small children who shares a massage office with a friend during the two full days during the work week that her mother is available to care for the children. Like Robert, she originally worked from home, but, recently decided to share an office not only to lessen the impact on her family's privacy, but to have a more professional environment and more easily gain exposure to a wider base of potential clients.

For Laura, this translates to a total of about 8 hours per week of paid massage (two days of three to five client hours each, sometimes a bit more or less), and another 8 hours or so per week of tasks related to doing those 8 hours of massage, i.e., time in between clients, doing laundry, client phone calls and emails, as well as some very basic marketing, client followup and record keeping work.

Laura and her partner both have family out of state that they visit a few times per year (for a total of about three weeks away from home and work), so with one additional vacation week beyond that, plus various school and religious holidays, assisting with an annual church retreat and other time away from the office (sick time for herself, her children or her partner), Laura estimates that she is only available for seeing clients about 40 weeks total per year.

As of this year, she's been able to keep her available appointments filled about 80% of the time; she lives in a small but economically prosperous town, has been in practice about three years, and currently feels comfortable charging $50 per hour for her primarily relaxation oriented massage work. She receives a few tips on top of that, but offers very few discounts and does not accept insurance.

Her expenses are low; her friend charges $150 per month, including utilities, massage supplies and the option to schedule her clients via her friend's website. Laura pays for her own association memberships and liability insurance; she does client laundry at home, and, deducts a small portion of her phone, laundry and internet expenses to reflect her cost of doing business as a massage therapist.

Earnings Worksheet – Case #2

A) Total hours available per work week: ___16___

B) Estimated administrative hours:
   approximately ½ of total hours (A): ___8___

C) Massage hours available per work week:
   Total hours (A) minus admin hours (B): ___8___

D) Work weeks available per year:
   52 weeks minus vacation, sick time,
   holidays, family time, etc. ___40___

E) Total potential massage hours per year:
   Massage hours per week (C)
   multiplied by weeks available (D): ___320___

F) Estimated percent of appointments filled: ___80%___ x .01 = __.80__

G) Adjusted massage hours per year:
   Total potential massage hours (E)
   multiplied by (F) ___256___

H) Estimated hourly rate for massage: ___$50.00___

I) Estimated Gross earnings:
   Adjusted massage hours (G) multiplied by
   Estimated hourly rate (H): ___$12,800.00___

J) Estimated Expenses and Taxes:
   Allow for one-third to one-half of
   gross earnings for expenses and taxes: ___$12,800/3 = $4267___

K) Estimated Net Earnings after taxes/expenses:
   Subtract Estimated Expenses/Taxes (J)
   from Estimated Gross Earnings (I): ___$8,533.00___

Case Study #3

Our third case study is about Ellen, who does both relaxation and treatment massage for a very diverse clientele four days a week for a total maximum of about 20 to 22 hours of hands on time. She lives in a medium sized town several hours from a large city, one that is known for summer recreational activities but that is also somewhat quiet in the winter due to potentially extreme weather conditions.

She rents a room in a quaint downtown building along with several other alternative practitioners, and spends another 20 to 25 hours a week doing a variety of unpaid but necessary tasks. She benefits from cross-referrals from the other practitioners in her building, and shares a website with them, but otherwise relies on relationship based strategies, word of mouth and community engagement for building and maintaining her practice. She does pay for an annual ad in the tourist focused town newspaper, and feels that this is a good investment for her business.

Ellen is single, has no children, loves to travel, and tries to schedules her travels so that she can also attend continuing education programs that are of interest to her. She usually plans to be out of the office between four and six weeks a year, and allows another two to three weeks for illness and/or unexpected events related to the weather in her area, particularly in the winter. She figures that she is available for massage approximately 45 weeks per average calendar year.

Ellen has just entered her sixth year of private practice and currently charges $70/hr, and plans to raise her hourly rate by $10 sometime within the next year or two. She offers very few discounts and does not accept tips for her work.

Overall, she estimates that she is currently able to fill about 85% of her available client hours. Her office rent is higher than most (but her clients love the ambiance and location), and she spends more on continuing education than most massage therapists might – and feels that both she and her clients benefit from her ever increasing knowledge base. She also pays for a laundry service, and, has her office professionally cleaned on a regular basis.

Earnings Worksheet – Case #3

A) Total hours available per work week: __44__

B) Estimated administrative hours:
   approximately ½ of total hours (A): __22__

C) Massage hours available per work week:
   Total hours (A) minus admin hours (B): __22__

D) Work weeks available per year:
   52 weeks minus vacation, sick time,
   holidays, family time, etc. __45__

E) Total potential massage hours per year:
   Massage hours per week (C)
   multiplied by weeks available (D): __990__

F) Estimated percent of appointments filled: __85%__ x .01 = __.85__

G) Adjusted massage hours per year:
   Total potential massage hours (E)
   multiplied by (F) __841.50__

H) Estimated hourly rate for massage: __$70.00__

I) Estimated Gross earnings:
   Adjusted massage hours (G) multiplied by
   Estimated hourly rate (H): __$58,905.00__

J) Estimated Expenses and Taxes:
   Allow for one-third to one-half of
   gross earnings for expenses and taxes: __$58,905.00/2__ = __$29452.50__

K) Estimated Net Earnings after taxes/expenses:
   Subtract Estimated Expenses/Taxes (J)
   from Estimated Gross Earnings (I): __$29,452.50__

Working For Other People

Given how many massage franchises, clinics, and other businesses have massage therapists working as independent contractors, we should also try to apply the earnings principles to those situations to the degree that that is possible.

You'll still have physical limitations as to how much massage you can do in a given period of time, but, the number of clients you see and how much you are paid will depend on the agreement you reach with the person or organization hiring you as an independent contractor.

You'll still pay your own local, state, and federal taxes (including self-employment taxes, but, the amount of unpaid administrative tasks that need to be done should decrease significantly depending on the exact situation in which you find yourself.

If doing massage for yourself means that your hourly rate is essentially halved (one hour of non-paid time for every paid client hour), then a "baseline" hourly rate for a massage therapist to use for comparison must include business expenses, but, not taxes.

So, for example, if a massage therapist in private practice charges $60 per hour of massage, that essentially means $30/hour (i.e., an hour of unpaid tasks for every hour of paid time with a client).

If you take an estimate 20% out for expenses (20% of $30 is $6), that's a pre-tax base rate of about $24/hour (again, not counting tips or discounts) - meaning that a spa or clinic should, in theory, be paying about that much to be competitive with what a massage therapist in private practice earns after expenses but before taxes.

Beyond that, if you can keep as busy working for other people as you can working for yourself (remember that 20 to 25 hour a week limit), then, getting paid around $24 per hour is roughly equal with working for yourself.

Summing Up

After reviewing (and, I hope, understanding) the basic earning principles that affect how much you can earn as a massage therapist and walking through some examples of how to apply those principles to different types of private practice situations, I hope you feel at least a little more confident in estimating your own earning potential as a massage therapist.

As you may already know, there's a lot more to earning a living as a massage therapist than just doing massage. There are a lot more well-written and useful books available now than there used to be, so I'm not going to try to write another book on material that's been so well-covered by others.

However, there are still lots of things to learn about (like the details of figuring out how much you can earn as a massage therapist!) that I haven't seen covered in detail anywhere else; knowing about these details can make understanding those larger books a lot easier.

Anyway, I've learned a lot since 1998, and I think some of what I've learned might be useful for other massage therapists, including, but not limited to:

- How Many Clients Do You Need for a Successful Massage Practice?

- Low-cost, Active Marketing Strategies for Long Term Client Retention

- Time and Task Management for the Solo Massage Practitioner

- Fueling the Massage Therapist: A Sports Nutrition Approach for Career Longevity

If you have any interest in these or other topics, please let me know, and, regardless, best of luck on your journey as a massage therapist!

Appendix A

Sample list of possible non-paid tasks for the solo practitioner

Ongoing/recurring unpaid tasks:

Basic self-care (breaks, food, walks, etc) in between clients (varies)
Return client phone calls/emails (0 to 30 minutes per day)
Keep office clean, water plants, dust, etc. (5 to 15 minutes per day)
Change sheets and tidying office in between clients (5 to 10 minutes per client)
Transport, launder and store sheets and other linens (varies with client load, can be minutes or hours per day/week)
Session/SOAP notes as required (varies)
Bank deposits and daily financial record keeping (5 to 30 minutes per day)
Schedule/reschedule clients before/after appointments(varies)
Manage client paperwork and insurance billing (varies)
Ongoing marketing projects and related followup
Gift certificate sales and tracking

Periodic unpaid tasks:

Massage done as a donation/gift/marketing tool
Thank you notes to new clients; birthday/holiday mailings to existing clients
Research and purchase office/massage supplies
Design/print marketing materials;website design/maintenance
Research/purchase advertising and commercial mass mailings
Research and create marketing projects/efforts as needed
Basic bookkeeping, reconciling bank and credit card statements
Tax preparation and payment
Research and attend continuing education
Professional and community meetings
Down time when clients forget/cancel at the last minute

Appendix B

Sample List of Possible Expenses for the Solo Practitioner

Regular/Recurring Expenses:

Office rent (may or may not include utilities)
Home office expenses (for those who practice from home)
Telephone (land line and/or cell phone)
Internet connection
Website hosting
Oils/lotions and other massage supplies
General office supplies, postage, laundry supplies

Periodic Expenses:

Liability insurance (general and for massage specifically)
Sheets, blankets and other linens
Professional books and publications
Continuing Education
Office furniture, massage table, computer
Professional association memberships
Chamber of Commerce membership
Advertising (print, internet, various other media)
Accounting and tax preparation
Vehicle expenses (mostly for mobile practitioners)
Local and state fees for massage licensing
Local and state fees for business license

Appendix C

Partial list of taxes that might apply to the solo practitioner:

Local taxes:

Cities, counties and other municipalities may have taxes that are required to be collected on personal services such as massage therapy.

Check with your local government to see what is required in your area.

State taxes:

Some states have an income tax, and may also require the collection and reporting of a Business and Occupation tax, as well as possible sales tax on personal services like massage, and/or property tax on any property you own for business purposes.

The Department of Revenue for your state will help you figure out what kind of tax collection and reporting is required in your state.

Federal Tax:

For massage practitioners with any amount income remain after business expenses, self-employment tax and Federal income tax will need to be estimated and paid on a quarterly basis.

Check with a tax adviser and/or the Internal Revenue Service for requirements that are specific to your overall financial and tax situation.

Earnings Worksheet

A) Total hours available per work week: _____

B) Estimated administrative hours:
   approximately ½ of total hours (A): _____

C) Massage hours available per work week:
   Total hours (A) minus admin hours (B): _____

D) Work weeks available per year:
   52 weeks minus vacation, sick time,
   holidays, family time, etc. _____

E) Total potential massage hours per year:
   Massage hours per week (C)
   multiplied by weeks available (D): _____

F) Estimated percent of appointments filled: _____ x .01 = ___

G) Adjusted massage hours per year:
   Total potential massage hours (E)
   multiplied by (F) _____

H) Estimated hourly rate for massage: _____

I) Estimated Gross earnings:
   Adjusted massage hours (G) multiplied by
   Estimated hourly rate (H): _____

J) Estimated Expenses and Taxes:
   Allow for one-third to one-half of
   gross earnings for expenses and taxes: _____ / _ = _____

K) Estimated Net Earnings after taxes/expenses:
   Subtract Estimated Expenses/Taxes (J)
   from Estimated Gross Earnings (I): _____